Carol Hamblen
304-598-5085

ANIMAL EYE

PITT POETRY SERIES
Ed Ochester, Editor

Animal Eye

Paisley Rekdal

University of Pittsburgh Press

Published by the University of Pittsburgh Press, Pittsburgh, Pa., 15260

Manufactured in the United States of America
Printed on acid-free paper
10 9 8 7 6 5 4 3 2

ISBN 13: 978-0-8229-6179-6
ISBN 10: 0-8229-6179-2

For my grandmother, Irene Stubbs, and for Sean

CONTENTS

Part I

Part II

Part III

Part IV

Part V

This life's dim windows of the soul
Distorts the heavens from pole to pole
And leads you to believe a lie
When you see with not through the eye.

William Blake, *The Everlasting Gospel*

PART I

Why Some Girls Love Horses

And then I thought, Can I have more
of this, would it be possible
for every day to be a greater awakening: more light,
more light, your face on the pillow
with the sleep creases rudely
fragmenting it, hair so stiff
from paint and sheet rock it feels
like the dirty short hank
of mane I used to grab on Dandy's neck
before he hauled me up and forward,
white flanks flecked green
with shit and the satin of his dander,
the livingness, the warmth
of all that blood just under the skin
and in the long, thick muscle of the neck—
He was smarter than most of the children
I went to school with. He knew
how to stand with just the crescent
of his hoof along a boot toe and press,
incrementally, his whole weight down. The pain
so surprising when it came,
its iron intention sheathed in stealth, the decisive
sudden twisting of his leg until the hoof
pinned one's foot completely to the ground,
we'd have to beat and beat him with a brush
to push him off, that hot
insistence with its large horse eye trained
deliberately on us, to watch—

Like us, he knew how to announce through violence
how he didn't hunger, didn't want
despite our practiced ministrations: too young
not to try to empathize
with this cunning: this thing
that was and was not human we must respect
for itself and not our imagination of it: I loved him because

I could not love him anymore
in the ways I'd taught myself,
watching the slim bodies of teenagers
guide their geldings in figure eights around the ring
as if they were one body, one fluid motion
of electric understanding I would never feel
working its way through fingers to the bit: this thing
had a name, a need, a personality; it possessed
an indifference that gave me
logic and a measure: I too might stop wanting
the hand placed on back or shoulder
and never feel the desired response.
I loved the horse for the pain it could imagine

and inflict on me, the sudden jerking
of head away from halter, the tentative nose
inspecting first before it might decide
to relent and eat. I loved
what was not slave or instinct, that when you turn to me
it is a choice, it is always a choice to imagine pleasure
might be blended, one warmth
bleeding into another as the future
bleeds into the past, more light, more light,
your hand against my shoulder, the image
of the one who taught me disobedience
is the first right of being alive.

Arctic Scale

after Subhankar Banerjee

The slides grow progressively red.
Now the black-and-yellow slicker encasing the man leans
like a ballet dancer across the animal, matching its length

and stretch, the strangely stiffened legs and slack head,
the man's knife already deep
inside the body.

He slits fat down to membrane
as muscle is exposed to air, the blue cells
brightening, gleaming

under plastic tendons the man massages then peels
carefully away.

There is no face.
But children appear in the following frame,
and now there is more red, the man and boys
taking apart the thickened blood that foams, one enormous jelly

pooling the snow so that rubber boots get wetted
up to the calf and what they touch

coats them utterly: there is no skin left, only
hands becoming intimate with the work,
cutting away horns and heart, tongue, lungs, kidney, liver,

scooping out intestines filled with grass
and placing them to the side, moving in
to the custard-colored musk nodes
bunched at the tail base, then further, looking
for whatever is left of use: what beats and swells
and stinks and pushes—

Now it's white
across which ant-like bodies of pregnant caribou

scatter in migration, photo shot
from the belly of a Cessna.

In the distance, mountain ranges

and the unseen sea to which they travel,
where the text below it announces
oil rigs dip their certain needles
and the Inuit women's breast milk has been declared
hazardous waste.

It is so beautiful here. Here is a wall-sized field of green
with patches of corn silk. Here is a miraculous range
seamed with what I have to be told is coal,
the enormous, glassy sea chattering its blue
to the sky, the glacier clasped between them
quietly disappearing.

Here is a view too big to stand or even read

the life inside: the slide clicks to an obscuring
shore of gray beside which water
churns with miniature baleens in knuckles of white.
Changes again. Abstracted fields

of snow and snow, and ice.

In the last, the man has left a flap
of caribou skin to dry.
It lies in a shrunken patch of snow, small
as a child's pink mitten
beside him; a valentine.

Ballard Locks

Air-struck, wound-gilled, ladder
        upon ladder of them thrashing
through froth, herds of us climb
        the cement stair to watch
this annual plunge back to dying, spawn;
        so much twisted light
the whole tank seethes in a welter of bubbles:
        more like sequined
purses than fish, champagned explosions
        beneath which the ever-moving
smolt fume smacks against glass, churns them up
        to lake from sea level, the way,
outside, fishing boats are dropped or raised
        in pressured chambers, hoses spraying
the salt-slicked undersides a cleaner clean.
        Now the vessels
can return to dock. Now the fish,
        in their similar chambers, rise and fall
along the weirs, smelling the place
        instinct makes for them,
city's pollutants sieved
        through grates: keeping fish
where fish will spawn; changing the physics of it,
        changing ours as well:
one giant world encased
        with plastic rock, seaweed transplanted
in thick ribbons for schools to rest in
        before they work their way up
the industrious journey: past shipyard, bus lot,
        train yard, past
bear cave, past ice valley; past the place
        my father's father once,
as a child, had stood with crowds
        and shot at them with guns
then scooped them from the river with a net, such
        silvers, pinks crosshatched with black:

now there's protective glass
        behind which gray shapes shift: change
then change again. Can you see the jaws
        thickening with teeth, scales
beginning to plush themselves with blood; can you see
        there is so little distinction here
between beauty, violence, utility?
        The water looks like boiling sun.
A child has turned his finger into a gun.
        Bang, the ladders say
as they bring up fish into too-bright air, then down again,
        while the child watches the glass
revolve its shapes into a hiss of light.
        Bang, the boy repeats.
His finger points and points.

The Orchard

Even in the dream he's old, returning from his shed
with a bucket of grubs he's picked off the roses.
Dead already these twenty years, in my dream
he moves steadily enough through the back field
landscaped clear to the power lines
that marched the length of Beacon Hill.
My grandfather tended an apple orchard there,
then set to making rows for sweet pea vines and tomatoes
though his wife complained of this cultivated Eden,
worrying it looked too "country" to the neighbors.
In the winter my grandfather ordered seeds
from a company out west, and all summer and partway
through fall sprayed the fruit with a thick mist
the catalogs recommended until, years later,
hard, berry-sized tumors grew in his pancreas
and his wife's small breasts. In the dream,
he wears one of the thin T-shirts he favored,
the raveled neck gone transparent at the seams,
below this a familiar pair of faded slacks—
"Mao-blue," my uncles ruefully called them—
bought in Beijing during the Reagan era.
He'd returned a final time to see his mother,
and for gifts brought back Mao jackets
and caps, Mao mailbags and figurines
my uncles and mother promptly buried
inside closets and dressers. On the fireplace,
the last, framed photos of his mother before
the children packed them off, the woman's shape
spidery with age, slim feet bound in black.
She died twice the summer he visited, the first
after a stroke from which she revived a day later
in the village's burial hut. My grandfather was good,
I remember, at fixing bicycles and making shelves,
he could replace a car clutch and once
devoted an entire basement wall to a series
of aquaria he'd built himself and stocked.

None of these interests did he pass on to his children.
He sat instead quietly through dinner,
fingering his dish of salted plums, slipping each
from its waxed wrapper to suck the meat to a pulp
full of the brined, tart juice of summer.
Though he wouldn't have been able to tell this
toward the end: the pesticides, the chemo
having poisoned his taste buds, perhaps his tongue—
For in the dream—as in my memories of him—
he remains speechless, one thin figure working
in the garden or basement, the neighbor's
hissed assessment of him filtered
through the juniper hedge he'd planted as a border
to gate our garden: *Such an odd man,*
he seems intelligent, though who can tell,
him unable to speak a word of English—
So that I was startled, years later, coming upon
his notebooks to find blazons of Chinese and English
blooming alongside photos of Depression-era girlfriends
clipped and pasted in satellite configurations
on black paper filigreed with white paint.
Curlicues of dragons' tails, emperors, rose trellises—
The English so carefully rendered, so perfectly phrased
that now, besides his secret art, it is my lack
of remembering this voice myself that most
disappoints, his silence renewed
in imagination that renders me similarly dumb.
In the dream, my grandfather holds out a box
filled with stamps torn off missives from Taiwan
and Russia, Denmark, Sweden, each one faded
yet folded carefully up, some in onionskin,
their water stains and ancient postmarks
like pressed flowers from a winter garden.
Whose stamps were these he wanted me to see?
Why did he believe such minutiae needed preserving?
I take the box, ignoring his long face looming

in a worry over my own, attracted by the sudden
Steller's jay that startles past his window.
I look, and the box slips from my lap, spills
its stamps like a spray of feathers from the bird
that has begun feasting now on the apples
in a corner of the orchard. Its dark head darts
into the branches for the fruit before the bird rises
again, flies off, its wings shuddering their streaks of blue
that fade into the darkness.

Flowers from a New Love after the Divorce

Cut back the stems an inch to keep in bloom.
So instructs the florist's note
enclosed inside the flowers.
Who knew what was cut
could heal again, the green wounds close,
stitching themselves together?

It doesn't matter. The flowers, red
and white, will bloom awhile, then wither.
You sit in an unlit room and watch
the vase throw crystal shadows through the dark.
The flowers' colors are so lovely they're painful.
In a week, you'll have to throw them out.

It's only hope that makes you take out scissors,
separate each bloom and cut
where you last measured. Did you know
Venus was said to turn into a virgin
each time she bathed? She did it
as a mark of love. She did it

so as to please her lovers. Perhaps,
overwhelmed by pain,
she eventually stopped bathing
altogether. It doesn't matter. It's a pleasure
to feel the green nubs stripped, watch the stems
refresh under your blade. They're here

because they're beautiful. They glow
inside your crystal vase. And yet
the flowers by themselves are nothing:
only a refraction of color that,
in a week or two, will be thrown out.
Day by day, the water lowers. The red-

and-white heads droop, blacken at the stems.
It doesn't matter. Even cut stems heal.
But what is the point of pain if it heals?
Some things should last forever, instructs
the florist's note. *Pleasure,*
says one god. *Shame,* says another.

Venus heads, they call these flowers.
In a week or two, you'll lose the note,
have to call the florist up.
With sympathy, you'll think he says.
Perhaps: *With love.* It doesn't matter.
You've stopped bathing. Alone,

you sit before the crystal
vase refracting you in pieces
through the dark. You watch
the pale skin bloom inside it, wither.
You petal, inch by inch.
You turn red and white together.

Possibilities in Love

I am so used to not clearly looking
that even the little ink drawing
on the wall of this restaurant
is a negation: the old king standing watch
over two young lovers,
only height marking one the hero,
the other his beloved.
While the dream etched inside her headpiece
opens like a window
onto an owl in winter, giving away her name,
Guinevere, the white wing of shadow.

The king has an absence in his breast.
It is a window, too,
which looks out onto a blue field with a girl
on a swing, not moving but watching,
solemnly, her entire world
a keyhole of green leading
up to the tiny mansion in which she must live.
The king's bone arm has been
denuded of flesh, fallen half
into death as the romance works itself slowly
to dust: his cool green eyes stare
at his wife, her lover, but cannot see
into each one's dream: hers,
the snow-white owl; his, the hummingbird
of vivid green feeding at a trumpet flower.

While under their wild, marvelous heads,
they too are bones and bones:
skeletons speckled with rich inks, dappled white
and pink like the carapaces of the crabs I've found
littered on shore all week,
the white sea pounding the stone beach,
white clouds, white horizon
that grows and swells only

so that it can later recede.
Possibilities in Love, the title reads,
and it is perhaps because of all these weeks of white
I suddenly want it: the details
so fantastic with its colors that don't dissolve,
the too-pink flesh, the too-green greenery,
that though this is not the first time
I have seen it, it is the first time
I have chosen to admire it,
feeling how it's been changed in me:
this patient accrual of detail that's become
a measure of belief if not beauty; that makes borders
and enframements where the horizon
only slips away.

I have walked all week
among houses built against and on top of
the bones of other houses, one era rewriting
the next, and seen kelp tangled in the broken
shells of clams and mussels, huge trees
stripped and rolled to shore, bits of Styrofoam
and sea-worn glass, strips of tire, a sheen
of oil, and once even the half-eaten body of a seal.
All of it evidence that the sea,
in its relentless working, makes equivalent.

But here, in this painting, the lovers
who lock themselves into the same gaze—faces
bridged by an iron clasp literally
pinning them by the chin—reveal
their differences: there is no transience, even
in this romance I keep imagining
in which a king gives away his wife to a man
too afraid to keep on wanting her.
Here, each figure wears an expression of refusal
in desire: he does not want to see the confession

of his wife. She can't unlock herself
from the gaze of her timid lover.
At the most, they want to formulate
a dream that might explain what it is
they will not, cannot be.

I have been sitting for hours inside this restaurant,
watching the sea outside break
and recede in white waves where fishermen
shout from the docks, cautiously navigating the cranes
that swing their cargo over ship railings,
each one the same size and color and shape,
as the men, too, in their upturned hoods
soften and blur, turn into the same man,
waving and waving.

A ferry turns its sleek side suddenly to the east.
As it starts to dock, the noon sun
glazes out its windows, one by one,
changing each from black to white, and then bright gold,
blanking out the passengers' faces with light,
blanking out the flagpole and metal railings
until I have to shield my eyes by raising up a palm,
until to see the thing at all
I have to stop looking.

Nightingale

The boy sits at the kitchen table
pointing through the window at the dark.
There is a bird that comes at night, he says,
that makes the most beautiful music.
Steam off the edges of the field, the gray
and brown and green of it, and beyond this, the sea.
What does he hear? I imagine
it is a nightingale, but have never heard one.
The look on the boy's face as he speaks
is the sound of a nightingale. It is the song
of a man strapped to his mast, straining
and tearing at the straps that bind him.
A small breeze moves off the sea.
It whistles over the shore, the dark
seal shapes that rock in and out
of the shoals. It hums there
till one of them turns long-necked, broken
and the clothes pull off like hair
as the divers drag the changed body
out of the sea. The field is wet and full of stars.
The boy cocks his head toward the dark.
I watch him moving back and forth
inside my vision, his body pieces of eye
and silk and arm and neck cord.
In the story, the man binds himself
so that he can listen. He wants to hear
the music that will pull him down.
He wants to put his head where the heart lives,
that small, hard singing behind a ribcage.
Night cuts down through the field. In spring,
the mists will burn off, the sea return bright green.
I have never seen such a live, dead thing before.
I think it is a nightingale. I tell the boy the name,
but he only smiles at me.
And yet, how is it not a nightingale?
Alone, the soft grunt of wings

beating behind me. I can sense its gold eye,
the throat encrusted with glass.
I can hear the water slapping
the white sides of the shore.
The boy stares out the kitchen window.
It hangs like a little square of cold before him,
a pane of shadow. The night outside this shadow
is black. The sea is distant. The bird,
however I imagine it, sings.

PART II

Wax

Family portrait with French Revolution and cancer

Tussaud is said to have knelt herself at the cooling bath
to mold him: Marat, "just after he had been killed

by Charlotte Corday. He was still warm, and his bleeding body
and the cadaverous aspect of his features presented a picture
replete with horror."

Now, the dripping head remains exactly

as it once looked, according to the placards, and to which
the famous painting can attest,

though what one says and what is history
are each rarely certain: here are only fragments

of what is left: the white sheet swaddling
the head, white body and bath, lank arm splayed
and the pallid face with its Egyptian cheekbones–

In the painting,
death comes in the form of a slight slit
delicately emblazoned on the right

pectoral: how tiny must have been that organ
for such a small wound to finish him. Not

like this wax man's heart, which must be large,
dangerous, intractable, worse than yours as the knife's great size
and placement indicate. Death

is not a small thing here. It takes work
to make it exact. It takes diligence.

Look, the doctors said,
as they took us in the room. *The new cells with the old ones.*
And they held the little chart up to the light.

ꝏ

Hands snatching in the plaster, the eye
sockets, lip cleft: all Tussaud could take back to reconstruct
cire perdue's inverse procedures: to coat the wax
on plaster instead, favor the viscous

over molten metals; Tussaud's uncle, Curtius, taught her,
taking out the little calipers and stylus, looking
at the body and only seeing it, stopping thought
in order to make it spectacle. "Curtius

has models of kings, great writers, beautiful women,"
noted Mercier. "One sees the royal family
seated at his artificial banquet—The crier calls from the door:

Come in, gentlemen, come see the grand banquet; come in, *c'est tout
comme a Versailles!*"

Come and look. The king
is seated by the emperor. He is just your size

though his clothes are finer, and now you see the long face
is less attractive than imagined, the crab-like hand curls
over plated fork and knife: you are so close, you can walk beside him,

pointing out the little similarities, the curved
and moistened lip, mild smile, fat pads
of the cheeks: all of it so close it hurts the eyes to pinpoint

just where the light is coming from, to give it shape,
distance by giving it a perspective altogether

different from yourself. *List all the family members
with a history of this condition.* Today,

ꙮ

on the first floor of Madame Tussaud's Wax Museum
you can find celebrities and sports stars, every politician of note
though you will not see these same figures five years in a row:

there is a death even for the deathless, objects
that depend on reputation to survive,

while the bodies in the chambered basement fever
in their blood-stained gowns. They can live forever

inside our terror, as in Florence, where once they sculpted
skeletoned ex-votos out of wax, oil-stained skins
appearing to stretch even as they stayed frozen, recalling Dante's belief
that the medium's malleability would retain whatever power

could be impressed upon it: a face, a ring, a life force.

It was a plague year. Churches
were filled with offerings: friezes of figures
writhing with disease, infants staked

in their parents' grips. The wax gives each body
illness' vivid texture, yellow skin, purple skin, skin that blackens
at the joints, all the colors corruption takes

as the bodies too collapse themselves to shelves
on shelves of flesh: the family become a single,

swarming mass of misery, as each ex-voto was itself
a prayer but altogether became a panic:
Take this shape, take this

body that is better than myself, that can be

burned down, melted, added to, can accrue
new filigree and detail: this one will survive
where the other won't. Look: the wax

shares our secrets of birth and age, but unlike us keeps renewal
stored inside the cells.

The doctors
took out their pens. They wrote down all the family
members with this condition: grandmother, grandfather,
aunt, uncle, father, mother, who

was it among us who hadn't been touched? There
the ring of candles smoking gold beside the casket.

And so we looked and looked, the mother's
father's face frozen in repose—

You have to look, the doctors said. And turned

ꙮ

the human into map, drew bodies that could be
chart and information traced through centuries of experiment.

How many bodies to make the one body, endow the corpse
with attributes of life?

To keep it mute, intemporal—

And so the medieval
manuscript's *écorchés* playing the lute, riding horses,
striding their bloodless legs into town. Here
one skeleton tilts a skull in his palm, his own bone face tilted toward us:

Genius lives on

while all else is material scrolled atop the vellum in its little,
withering snicker: it is all material here: all

answer and answer for the doctors,
and when the manuscript wasn't enough they scraped
the hive's glass scales with a knife.

They pounded and shaped, they took skulls
and poured on paraffin for skin
to give the blank bone personality again.

The wax could go where the mind was stuck.
It abandoned the map.

You're
a visual person, the doctors said. *Imagine this,*
and pointed to a color, a stain, an opening.

I'd needed more and so they gave me more. They made
an anatomy of me.

ꟹ

In the museum, families want to take their pictures
with the murderers. They pace
the chamber's cavern to stare into black pockets
of shock, cave after cave:

it was Tussaud who thought to bring in the death,
though hadn't it always been here?

Here is the killer with his handsome face.
Here is Manson, Bundy, Hitler,
the Terror's row of heads still spiked on stakes:

you can see into the cavern

of the jaw, and what is that feeling
its way out through the neckhole, these dead

of the dead, these never-dead,
where to look disperses what we think we see
the second it enters us?

The world is all brain, and does it matter that the thing before us
is a replication?

Even the wax only holds its breath—

And here is pancreas and breast, ovary, uterus, veins

that spangle fragmentary ropes, a negative
of this view outside my window where snow
on the hills creeps downward, turns fall trees in their fog beauty
necrotic, ghost.

The code, simply, degenerates. On a table,

ℵ

the head of Robespierre, Fouquier de Thinville.
They are here still, some personality crawls

like an animal into its tiny hole, fits itself there, invites us in,
then repels us: back, back: we are the kings here still and you

cannot join us, and when they marched the busts of the ministers
from Curtius's house ("They demanded," he wrote Tussaud, "insistently
the citizens"), the busts were burned, were violently attacked.

The real has no limits, and still, is full of limit.

We think the heart matters. We think the breath,

too, and they do, that is what the wax says, and then
denies it: you are a king, too, and if you have loved him so long
by his symbol, here is something more exact.

Otherwise, why keep a real

guillotine crouched in the corner, why real
period clothes, real blood-stained shoes, no glass
so that when you go to the bathroom later
you are surprised to see the face in the mirror

twist into its expressions?

And the long corridors opened, and the doctors moved their hands
across my mother's breasts, her hips, they marked on charts the places
that were familiar. We used to joke

about the pesticides her father used, little silver canister swinging
at his hip. You could hear how close he was
in the garden by that panicked clatter, the stupid
immigrant. The tomatoes were silver after he'd finished.

And the radiation after X's polio. And the pills
the doctors pushed for Y. And the chemicals with which they infused
our napkins, our pencils, our mattresses, our milk—

☙

Look how the wax imbibes our novelty and richness.
It takes on some of our power as well, the blood paint
of the Christ statue seeming
to run, to swell. For centuries they argued

how to divide him, man or God, till Calenzuoli shaped
a wax man's head then split the face
to find it: scalp flayed over the intact portion of his crown, flesh halo

where the passive gray eyes flicker and the stripped muscles gleam.

What is man is all red and red, tendon, cartilage
glimmering with a sheen of beef fat,
while the rest is the expression

of a patience endured through pain: our image
of the image of Christ, the exactness
of his interiority, the wet formulations of the mind.

"Eye, nose, lip / the tricks
of his frown, his forehead; nay,
the pretty dimples of his chin and cheek—

Would you not deem it breath'd? And that those veins
did verily bear blood?"

ꙮ

I had noticed that they took
certain patients' families into a room
during the operations. Separated them
from where the others waited,
so it was obvious when the doctors came
and led a group into the little room, and shut the door.

You could hear the muffled something, the scuttle
in the dark that signaled pain,

which was why I began to sing, *It's fine,*
during the operation, cheerful, witless, *It's fine, it's fine,*
so long as they don't take us into that little room

which is what they did, three hours later, the doctor
and his trout-faced resident.

We have some news,
the doctor said, and as the door shut my father
turned to me with a look that read,
I will never forgive you.

So many models, so many bits of grotesquery—

In the museum is Robert Francois Damiens who,
in 1757, was ordered to have his flesh ripped

with pincers and, by proclamation, "on those places poured
molten lead, boiling oil, resin, wax,
body quartered by horses, his limbs consumed by fire."

The portrait of this pain, in its own way, a kind of compliment.

To make this man's suffering significant because
prohibitive, because

it would be the most intense form of privacy imaginable.

They tortured a person

out of the body that they killed, and then they changed this:
Guillotin remodeling the blade to sculpt the new
blood-wet window through which his "patients"
would look. To turn each death anonymous, communal—

"Passenger," wrote Robespierre's epitaph, "lament not his fate,
for, were he living,
thou would'st be dead." Insert yourself

inside this window. Crowds
pushing against soldiers, shrubbery, platforms, crowds
looking and feeling at another
just like themselves.

I am a man because I suffer,
the thin gas voice leaks inside the chamber, or is it,

I am a man because I make others
suffer in my place?

☙

How much *enough* to call it evidence?

I thought my father would faint when he heard the results.

The insides seamed as if with. The diamond of the flesh turned into,
turned out of, it was hard to tell.

You have to imagine, the doctors said.
To spend an afternoon combing these words. To walk

among the white pillars of the Temple of Poseidon
looking for the name some poet etched there once
as a kind of afterthought, rows and rows
of white stone, and no one could find it:

so many others had added names, dates, the pillars
had become a kind of cemetery,

but I was desperate for the remnant, the authority.
I needed to trace my fingers through the name, to step inside of it.

How deep the eye. How deep the knife, the hand, the imagination—

And once again we took off
coat and sweater, blouse and skirt. Someone came
and washed her scent off. The oils of her hair.

How much further and still be her?
They put a knife in. They took out lining
and consciousness, tissue, time, they took out speech,
then brought it back. And now

they give us another body, a littler one, and we start
the process over in reverse. The lenses, blouse, shoes, skirt,
makeup, hair oils. And added to it, the little
rubber breast padding for what's been lost—

I should have looked, like Tussaud, with my glasses
and my lock of hair.

I should have stood stretching out my hand for the perspective,
knowing it was only a thought that night that I

was the killer, I had the knife in hand, I was taking out the heart
and tongue, I was cutting off the fingers, it was me doing it,
that blood, that distance—

Nothing scraped at the floorboards. Nothing blew down and whistled
in the street. And somewhere an image
in the mind's blank cavern: the body's senseless

clawing out of color, its muds and greens and pallid lights.

You cannot tell just what the body is
or where the corruption will take it:

it is like trying to pinpoint the soul
as it animates the body: it exists, like a painting does,

between the real and imagined, where the wax itself
comes back to life.

They asked us to look
and understand the stain, the shadow on the x-ray
but the shadow was too much a shape

to be an idea as yet. We looked, and the shadow
turned into fist, a face, it blossomed
like a Japanese lotus in a dish of water, it turned
beautiful and remote, black sun around which
the ghostly others lost duration, turned themselves in orbit—

No, the doctors said. And urged us to paint

the image thickly over, keep her untouched color
and shade, hue that recalls the vivid flesh
and just its opposite, to let dirt scrub into the cracks—

After the operations, she is
not only human but the state
of working toward humanity, away from it,

while in my mind her face can be remolded to last
longer than wood, longer than stone, to last

as long as there is wax, her image always at the point
of just emerging. Let me look. Here

are the cells with their rotten codes.
Here are breasts, belly, the still-pink organs ripe and flush:

myself liquifying into the family's
deathless increase.
I can see the swelling
in armpit, groin, the milk glands ripened in the breast. Passenger:

I had no idea what it meant,
lingering alone, black-eyed in doorways—

Take off the vest. Peel off the fragments
that are left, the sweat-stained
shoes and blouse, glasses, sweater: let us trace our fingers
through the names, let us add them to us, so that later
we can take it all away.

The drumroll is echoing in the chamber. It takes me down

where so many have gathered, crowds upon crowds
for the blood-wet window
through which each citizen must look.

The crowd shudders as the cord is cut. Shock
that travels through everybody. Makes a family out of every
body. Then isolates the patient.

They held my little x-ray up to the light and.

The king is dead. Do you believe it?

Passenger: touch this pillar for a sign.

Someone has to raise the head.
Someone has to imagine the other side.

PART III

Voyeurs

A horse falls on a girl
in its trailer. The horse
is a thoroughbred
lame with founder. The girl
a girl. You can't
imagine the pain.
You can't
because this story
isn't yours, isn't that
of the woman telling it
either. You watch
her take the basket
of bread, tear it
slice by broken slice.
When the horse
slips in the moving
trailer, it pins the girl
by her torso to the floor.
The woman smiles.
If he tries to rise,
she says, his shoulder
will push downward
to her spine. The dull
thud of the heart
beats against her chest.
She orders another
glass of wine.
You can see
the girl's damp fingers
stroke the silken neck.
You can't imagine why
the woman looks at you
and smiles. The horse
will grind its full weight
into her. In the light,
your thin sleeves sway

like flame. An image
of the time he grabbed
your wrist, twisted
till you cried
that he would break it.
The woman takes the smallest
sip of wine.
Her face is flushed.
A lock of hair is caught
inside your mouth.
One quick twist
of shoulder. Another
glass of wine? Voices
sweep the metal, echo
through the trailer. What
to say of the dim shapes
moving in the dark?
Straw rustles. The breath
grows shallower. You watch
the damp face twist, the hands
reach out to tear
another, broken slice.

Body of Stuffed Female Swift Fox, Natural History Museum

Nothing ever was this slinking, vicious,
glass eye embedded in its slitted red, skin
husked and sealed forever in a vacuum:
the false gray sedge where no dog hunts
and it's lost its sleekness as it's lost its sun.

She ages terribly behind glass.
Nothing ever was this slinking, vicious,
so why should we admire or hate her,
husked and sealed forever in a vacuum,
the frozen attitude of cunning

strung over wire, razor nails replaced
and aging terribly behind glass?
Imagine the wounds she could tear into a body.
Why admire or hate her for them,
why not call her existence, simply, honest:

an animal practicing its craft designed by nature?
Now she's strung over wire, the razor nails replaced
with plastic as her forest was itself replaced
by us, the many wounds we've torn into its body.
Years ago, signs across the neighborhood

listing all the cats found mutilated declared
a man was busy practicing his craft, nature redesigned
by violence. We have to find the killer, they said,
before the forested park fills with bodies,
the cats turned into girls and the girls into women.

Months later, the signs were torn down, the notices
listing all the cats found mutilated declared
a mistake. The culprit was a fox. Now, behind glass
we've found the killer: the violence
we think we cannot be or feel more than,

the once-red body that fascinates us
labeled female, the signs beside it torn, notes
on its habitat in disarray due to construction.
The culprit is a fox. Behind glass
lighting flickers, throws down shadows so that

we cannot see her. She raises up a paw
and the once-red body that fascinates us
freezes in its shabby immortality, stands disfigured
in its habitat, in disarray due to our construction
of a world that keeps her always different from us;

in our imagination of ourselves, degraded.
We cannot see her. She raises up a paw
as if in supplication, cone nose tasting the air
frozen in its shabby immortality, disfigured
by the box we've locked it in, as we've locked in her,

imagining how she'd slip from the forest to drink
at a puddle of rain, the vision of herself degraded
by a car's headlights that cut across its surface.
She lifts her head, cone nose tasting the air
and the wind lifts too, riffling the grasses, the trees,

the fur at her throat; a movement that,
as she stops to drink at her puddle of rain,
could be herself, the wind, or nothing: an absence
in the headlights that cut across the surface.
She looks into her puddle of rain

but will not imagine more, does not need to, like us,
a wind riffling through grasses, a movement
like water running down a glass room.
Nothing ever was this slinking, vicious.
She could be herself, the wind, or nothing. Instead,
she's husked, red. Sealed forever in a vacuum.

An Enemy

the mother says, and there it stands, rooted
where its ice-white tentacles wave:
pink-mouthed, voluptuous anemone

sinuous as the octopus that hangs
from the same cramped crag, undulant head
a fragile-skinned testicle one

ribbon arm strokes gently
while it sleeps. So I have found myself

with a protective arm tucked
between the legs: even in sleep I have my enemies,

waking this week in the house of a girlfriend
who hates me, and dreaming
of some strange shape slipped from the sea that peers
and pries the leafy dark,
pushing forward to surround me—

                              Bat rays shadow the surface of the tank
through coves of orange-cupped coral; sea pens and sunflower stars,
frilled kelp maroon as cabbage peel where parents

point out features that will thrill: this fish with a face

wider than a child's, that with its snout
shaped like a needle, another with a set of canine teeth
so sharp one father has to reassure
his little girl, *Don't worry: they don't like*

the taste of humans, though what animal,
famished, death-pressed, can't learn? The octopus

is quick enough to pick a lock, fits through

anywhere it slips its beak, triple-hearted: it will blush
sunset to wound, slippery

underarm silks billowing like sleeves
or tightened to a knuckled fist
that could tear a woman's hair back from the nape.

Absurdly flexible, it skirls
through grays and pinks
of rippled light, while in the Outer Reef
kelp shudder, plummet in plumes
that make their very changeableness

nauseating. The water plunges, sucks
as we watch and sway.

There's an ocean trapped inside the room—

My friend prefers to stand
by small displays, stare through magnifying glasses
at the barely visible: secret,
chemical worlds like those she might sniff out on the sleeve
of her husband's shirt. She waves me up to see

the clumsy, obvious aggressions
of creature living beside creature: as in the Learning Room
where groups of boys shriek

and plunge their hands in tide-chilled pools
of starfish, mussel; scrape buckles
on cemented shale. It's almost a relief

to find the hermit crab
so containable; discover the inverted, convex glass
is what distorts, shrinks the skate

and saw-shaped sturgeon, turns blimp-sized sea bass
pug-shaped, blunt; the scaled rosettes
in tiny bloom.

You can see the accuracy, if not the truth
of their design, like the mother's face
that, in the glass beside me, looks proud as the moon.

She has a lovely little girl. And that fish has a name

I'll never mispronounce.
An enemy, she repeats, *how great*, and delights
as her child, reaching in the endless bowl of light,

tumbles into space—

Happiness

I have been taught never to brag but now
I cannot help it: I keep
a beautiful garden, all abundance,
indiscriminate, pulling itself
from the stubborn earth: does it offend you
to watch me working in it,
touching my hands to the greening tips or
tearing the yellow stalks back, so wild
the living and the dead both
snap off in my hands?
The neighbor with his stuttering
fingers, the neighbor with his broken
love: each comes up my drive
to receive his pitying,
accustomed consolations, watches me
work in silence awhile, rises in anger,
walks back. Does it offend them to watch me
not mourning with them but working
fitfully, fruitlessly, working
the way the bees work, which is to say
by instinct alone, which looks like pleasure?
I can stand for hours among the sweet
narcissus, silent as a point of bone.
I can wait longer than sadness. I can wait longer
than your grief. It is such a small thing
to be proud of, a garden. Today
there were scrub jays, quail,
a woodpecker knocking at the white-
and-black shapes of trees, and someone's lost rabbit
scratching under the barberry: is it
indiscriminate? Should it shrink back, wither,
and expurgate? Should I, too, not be loved?
It is only a little time, a little space.
Why not watch the grasses take up their colors in a rush
like a stream of kerosene being lit?
If I could not have made this garden beautiful

I wouldn't understand your suffering,
nor care for each the same, inflamed way.
I would have to stay only like the bees,
beyond consciousness, beyond
self-reproach, fingers dug down hard
into stone, and growing nothing.
There is no end to ego,
with its museum of disappointments.
I want to take my neighbors into the garden
and show them: Here is consolation.
Here is your pity. Look how much seed it drops
around the sparrows as they fight.
It lives alongside their misery.
It glows each evening with a violent light.

Feel Like a Little Trepanning Today?

Imagine how much better we'd sleep
without breathing. How perfect we might seem
could we shake out human excess
like flotsam from a purse, pare down the design
from our mistakes: the gall
stones, appendices all on display to indicate
how what works remains enmeshed
with what resolutely doesn't.
The intrinsic might be

just what we don't need, like consciousness, say,
or childhood diabetes, all the pent-up energies
of this thing we call *the soul*.
Instead, how busily we play
at erasing ourselves: the eye
bags, the carnivals; scraping faces
baby-smooth out of desire's
putative, feral needs. Here,
a waft of memory goes up
like a tossed scarf, like what someone once said was smoke—
but no, not like smoke, not like smoke at all—

I think the soul snuggles down with the cerebellum and rouses
tired of itself. I think the soul, complete
in its knowledge of the body,
would prefer fewer things to imagine
cut out, sewn up, perfected, *dead*.
The seamlessness of a brain lain naked
in blue cloud, cradled in its skull of wind—

What we know
is that the frivolities we depend on most
can't embed themselves; remain. But what we fear
is another kind of change: that difference
simmers in the very flesh, experience

curdled into thought that tears us,
slowly, into self-
aware parts. So tonight
a woman thinks, *What now*?
before the unflattering glass,
while the one she loves, behind her, grins,
and asks himself, *Who else*?

Tango Lesson

The point is not to give yourself away but to connect
as closely as you are able to

your partner's will in the embrace, so that intent
slides seamlessly through two

sets of veins, one chest following the movement
of the next without break, heads fused

delicately at the temple till the other's perspiration
trickles down your face.

Observers think the dance is all improvisation
but they're wrong: each step must trace

its pattern: only empathy and good timing
in the sacada keep you from getting kicked

or trod on. The follower must mime
back her leader's embellishments in slick

gestures that articulate each pause. She should wear
black if possible, and master every subtle

twist of knee or leg since hips won't do here, pleasure,
for once, being located in the ankle.

Some complain about the rules. If that's you,
learn how the music in each milonga

changes; school yourself to understand a tune's
interplay of discipline and form; follow along

as Gardel's 1920s rigid eights slip in the '60s with Solare,
to hear how a single note might soar

above the beat that locks a couple into step,
    loosening the bond between dance and dancer

so that imagination, for the moment,
    can enter the feet.

So many tanguero novices freeze
    in place because they can't keep

track of any difference in beat.
    You see their terrified clutches

in dance halls all across the city, the leaden feet
    and sagging bellies of those who lose their axis

and lean too heavily on a partner.
    By the end, they barely can recall

the steps for their part. Tin-eared,
    they stand or shuffle in boxes,

moony, four-legged, with two separate hearts.

Intimacy

How horrible it is, how horrible
that Cronenberg film where Goldblum's trapped

with a fly inside his Material
Transformer: bits of the man emerging

gooey, many-eyed; bits of the fly
worrying that his agent's screwed him—

I almost flinch to see the body later
that's left its fly in the corner, I mean

the fly that's left its body, recalling too
that medieval nightmare, Resurrection,

in which each soul must scurry
to rejoin the plush interiors of its flesh,

pushing through, marrying indiscriminately
because Heaven won't take what's only half:

one soul blurring forever
into another body.

If we can't know the boundaries between ourselves
in life, what will they be in death,

corrupted steadily by maggot,
rain, or superstition, by affection

that depends on memory to survive?
People should keep their hands to themselves

for the remainder of the flight: who needs
some stranger's waistline, joint problems,

or insecurities? Darling,
what I love in you I pray will always stay

the hell away from me.

PART IV

Easter in Lisbon

I can't see why I come back to this,
Gaçar, Cinqo, Moarcar,
Alma: all the neighborhoods of Lisbon's

pale outline half-dismembered
by a spring fog rising by the zoo
I'd visited alone for pleasure:

one grudging kiss before the blue
Real Turismo bus swallowed you back up,
to return you home to London where you

were, that year, like me reading Trollope—
Another exchange student in a Trinity
slum that was at least a step up

from the usual arrangements. The projects, you told me
once, just south of L.A., which now
were burning. That spring, Rodney King

was everywhere on the news and how
we were the Great North American Failed
Experiment, as one Portugese student showed

us shyly, shaking out his paper's translation
at a local café. We'd met
that break to travel together, *just as friends*,

we said, though each night we slept
in the same bed and every day
we grew closer, your hand slipped

around my waist in the market fray,
my head tipping against
your shoulder on the train—Never to say

what it was we wanted, embarrassed
by such elaborate subterfuge, the stakes
of mere desire raised so high you'd speak

about a violent past in order to stave
off more attraction between us,
shake loose any tentacles of affection

that could bind. You got out of South L.A. because
you lived on the fringes of its border: it helped seeing
something different than death; unlike your friends,

it kept you from the needles
and guns you liked to brag about: horrors
I'd never seen and couldn't imagine,

a girl so boorishly middle class
her parents hadn't even divorced.
You knew me then as one who used

passivity to be liked, so in your lectures
you indulged yourself completely
till I had sense enough to argue

back, to rage against your rage,
until we finally ran out of money.
We fought; we parted. Alone, Easter eve, I trudged

the rain-soaked city blocks from Lisbon's
misty centrum to its zoo to comfort myself
by watching the insane wolf pace in its ruined

cage, fur rubbed loose in foam-
colored tufts, while four mottled penguins
sulked together on a stone.

It was, without a doubt, the worst zoo
I'd ever witnessed: nothing but discolorations
of shit and mildew; a raw, rank stink and ooze

permeating the air from cages
left uncleaned, from animals no one seemed to think
needed attention so much as space

and time to be alone. The sun bear coughed.
The single bonobo had mange.
So imagine, then, my delight at coming upon the rough-

hewn menagerie filled with lively parrots
and lemurs placed near the empty river trough
built for a once-living hippopotamus.

I stood before its giant, iron-barred dome watching
the frantic green dart of parrots
arrowing bar to bar, gold-red bodies

scrabbling in play, hopping across
each others' backs or poking fingers
through the bars to pierce the monotonous

gloom of the place, screeching at each other
in delight. At least *this* place was colorful,
one small shard of life in the drear

and yeasty gray of the city, and so I let it all
wash over, this tumbling feast
of greens and reds; not seeing for several

minutes that the lemur adults
were using their infants like little vacuums
from the cage: small enough to sneak

between the bars, the infants (bruisingly
tight grips kept upon their tails by the moms)
were pushed toward the walk to seek out food:

bits of popcorn, candy, gum, numbly
shoving what they could into their open
mouths, at which point the adults yanked them

back, tearing the leftovers
from between their teeth, then
devouring it themselves. Over

and over this occurred, a scene
I found both hideous and absurd,
unable to stop myself from laughing

at the animals' cruel intelligence:
foolishly I pulled out the orange
I carried in my purse

to offer as a treat, only to find the foragers
utterly surrounding me, a dozen tiny lemurs lured
out by the promise of fresh food. One rummaged

at my jeans and began spitting until, with a blurt
of fear at its sudden leaping
for my arm, I tossed the orange under

a bush, watched the infant scamper greedily
after. As if on cue, the cage emptied of all its littlest
occupants: upon the pavement, bodies

rushed and tumbled, twisting
out of their parents' grasps to flout
their newborn freedom. I froze in position

as the lemurs flooded down and out,
ignoring my open purse
entirely in their desperation to escape,

to be *outside*, the parrots cursing
from their perch while a sleep-dazed
guard paused in his walk to nurse

a casual smoke. He didn't even look our way
as half the tiny animals slipped
down the path, scampering in play

over the chain-link fence that
separated them from the Herpetarium.
The mothers hooted, the parrots spat

out cries of outrage while I slunk back,
hoping no one had witnessed this minor revolt I'd led
by the snack bar. Behind me, a thicket

rustled, unveiling a peacock, which is when
I saw the sign just behind in black and blocky
English text which read:

Warning. Do not feed monkeys.
And then, lower down, **Next stop**
Tiger. This Way. *Fuck me*

if I'm going there, I thought,
walking shakily back to the entrance.
Who knew what shock

waited around the corner, panting
in its flimsy cage, this time ringed
with chicken wire, perhaps; a fence

composed entirely of string?
After an hour, I'd done enough.
I was tired and hungry. It was the morning

of Easter eve, everyone else was in a rush
of cooking or wrapping presents,
everyone but me, flush

with time but no more money, distant
by thousands of miles from home
and nostalgic for some sense

not of the past but some vaguely imagined
future I might share with a person
like yourself. Erstwhile intimate,

I wanted you to see this with me, unable to explain
the terms on which we'd parted: the fact
of our attraction and our fear of it, afraid

not just of the simple act
of love itself, the brave face
put on desire's impulses, the slipknot

of monogamy itself—No, I admit
I was afraid of you, yourself,
what I imagined must constitute

your *blackness* (how help-
less does that word seem now, how stupid).
No, fear didn't teach me this, but self-

righteousness perhaps, the brute
attempt to seem less racist than simply practical:
we both believed that race was some crude

instinct to divide and divide, fanatical
separation that personal experience only
enabled further. Indeed, I'd be delusional

to natter on about desire when I'd seen
it ignored beside the fact of us, the tireless
looks we generated across Europe: your black knee

against my white one, the way the madam at the pensione
clucked her tongue at our shared sleeping
arrangement and, in one exaggerated flourish I can't begin

to mimic, swept out all the money
from my hand without once touching my skin.
The widow in black who screamed

at us on the street, or the border guards
who took you and the African traveling
that day into the small room off the train yard

to question you, refusing your release
until, hours later, you returned to me, hard-
faced to the border station we'd been

stranded at: midnight at the very lip
of Portugal, a town so small it had only one street
lamp left burning: one flickering blip

of powder yellow that illuminated
my face, then yours, in sulfur strips.
All this, and then in Lisbon, the amazement

of the Africans. By day, they'd watch our trips
to the market or museums,
but at night they'd come to you, to us, to slip

their hands in yours, staring at your *new*
milk color, as one man called it, his
own blue-blackness nearly bleaching you

out by comparison, murmuring
over your jeans, your bag, your shoes,
transmutable fascination shivering

like a coil of electricity between you
whenever he caught your eye, he wondering
what might become of him, too,

could he leave; you wondering what would
have been yours could you have stayed. Two
days before, we'd stood

at the edge of Spain, in Malaga,
looking out toward Morocco, its gray hood
just rising from the sea, an Africa

you laughed off as a dream so near
it seemed impossible, a Saharan
nightmare, perhaps, a land that could never

be what you most needed or preferred.
Instead, you stood on the sea walk's ruined stair
and promised yourself *Later,*

wandering disconsolately back to our bare
hotel. But later was only more
Spain, Portugal, your acquaintances coming to stare

at you each night, their first American African, to pour
over the translated intricacies
of a family past, to look at me, and to admire

you even more. Or no: that wasn't
admiration in their glance now, was it?
Rather than smile at me, they grimaced:

one detail from our trip you overlooked,
posing with a heavy arm draped across
my shoulder. Quite a change from that

warning look you shot me when I lied in Dover
about us being married. I remember that
you said—after the incident at the border—

you survived by going blind at crucial moments.
Had you allowed yourself to see it all, the stares
and insults, the widow's treatment

of us on the streets, then years
ago you'd have gone insane. Spent,
what more could you believe or bear?

We knew that it was never shyness that kept us
prudish, sweaty-palmed for weeks the news
droned on and on and Rodney King was beaten

again on flickering TVs from Lisbon to the English mews,
people charging through the streets, Korean
groceries burning on every corner, the grainy news

video replayed in which we saw pictures of police
officers, their thin arms raised
with clubs, descending swiftly,

over and over. Those wretched months, you hated
the British papers where we lived,
their claims that we were a nation that thrived on rage,

a collection of the most inhuman savageries: our failure
being inevitable since, by our own volition,
we were a people enamored only of the future—

Banded together by such ignorance,
how could the U.S. not brutally dissolve?
Of course, now I see why I come back to this:

Easter, Lisbon, all the animals
rotting in their cage: but let me say
we were never just our national

story—no one can be that painfully
reductive—though we were, perhaps, not without
its context. We were two people who prayed simply

to see ourselves as apart
from this obscene symbolism
we'd been made into, that we'd in part

made out of each other, emblems forever latent
in this poem's opening, a racism we've worked
into our language that twists imagery out of imagery, the tale

quietly doubled with each syllable it's spoken—
Apt metaphor for love itself, but it really
isn't love I'm speaking of, except perhaps the token

love of self, the self's need for an objectivity
that helps it survive. What were we doing in Portugal
but trying to change but also keep

some deeper part of us intact, the secret self
you saw in me as well, your compliments:
"I love your almond eyes, the spice I smell

coming from your skin,"
or "I think of you as my little China doll"?
Wondering aloud if my thin

skin was the result of my Chinese
or my Norwegian parent. And though this non-
whiteness might have been enough to tease

out some bond between us at home,
in Europe it became another
weapon to be used, to make me harm-

less in comparison, more
consistently an objet d'art
even than a white woman, something far

more delicate, more exotic locked at the heart
and pacing in its cage.
I was something to be protected in part,

in part to be used. Did you ever gauge
how much your desires mimicked
those of the ones you hated?

Regardless, I understand our machinations
sixteen years later: how you liked
my fear, your self-flagellations

of rage designed to make me feel spite-
ful, awkward, guilty. I was right to
resist loving you. And you were right

to take what advantage that you could
of me. Still, it meant we were,
as the student translated

for us, the Great North American
Failed Experiment, with all its cracks and latent
seepages, all its barbarian

insecurities. So now if clarity of vision
might drain away rage,
I ask you, Tell me what you see. Explain

your landscapes of Spain, Portugal;
rewrite the details that frustrated
and finished us. Tell me about that terrible

zoo you never visited, its bright spray
of lemur bodies running
from their cage to escape into the gray

and fog-drenched city,
this time inciting in their desire
all the other animals to flee,

the parrots and the sun bear,
the penguins languishing on their stone.
Fang and claw, fur and feather,

all of them rushing past the gates, down
the path leading into town
to dissolve into the backdrop of Lisbon's

neighborhoods, where a man and woman
sit at home; above them, a son asleep.
Now they turn at a motion

by their window to see a tiger
slipping past them on the walk: its stripes,
against the dark gold hide and white underfur,

like black icicles; its pink mouth glassy, opened wide.
The couple starts, the tiger stalls,
and now they stare at each other, eye

to eye, animals to animal,
struck dumb not by fear of each other
so much as the *unlikeliness* of it all.

The tiger rubs its chalk-white chin upon its paw,
then turns away again, its bright,
self-protective gaze, its black, retractable claws;

as more mist suddenly descends upon the house's gate
and the tiger slips back into its fog—
black and gold, and black and white—

leaving the couple to watch night fall:
to sit before their mirrorlike window,
frozen, speechless, and awed.

PART V

A Small, Soul-Colored Thing

The dog walked out of the forest with the deer in its mouth.
No. The deer came out of the forest. The dog
ran beside it, over, under: the dog slipped itself
into the animal lurching to my side of the road,
one of its throats bent back to the sky,
one of its spines dissolved to pear-white belly.
The throat was red. And the long legs looked broken.
But I made a mistake. The legs were not broken.
And the deer did not appear dead, though it must have been,
animated by the dog's hunger so that the deer moved
when the dog did, shivered like the soul inside the body,
the dog's face all red, which could be the color of the soul.
The back of the dog was sleek and brown
and expensive looking. When I stared at him,
I could see the lawns he must have escaped from,
the gravel drive winding down from the hills in the gold tags
jangling at his chest; the clean, pink flaps of his ears
flushed with cold. Now they were froth covered.
And his eyes were glazed with a furious longing.
The dog tore at the deer's throat as if he could dig
himself inside of it. The dog became a dog
again, and I watched him do it, and the deer became
something else: it left the soft ash shape of the doe
grazing by the bus stop, it abandoned
the buck's bright energy leaping over the stone wall
that separates my house from the cemetery,
its low border taut as a muscle that herds of deer trace
in moonlight, cast out of the canyons choked with snow.
The deer became some shadow torn between us:
beneath it, the beautiful legs, the elegant ribs
twisted into the road. I stopped and watched
this wrestling, the dog half deer, the deer
half dog, myself poised behind them
so as to remain invisible, though a low,
slow growl loosed itself at my approach.
It entered the deer and reverberated there

until its fur grew long and thickened,
and its face took on the shape of a lion,
a wolf, a bear. It became the shape of a mouth
tearing and tearing as I watched it, wanting
to take my share of it, kneeling at the walk
and putting my mouth to the flesh, letting
fur and blood both coat my tongue, while my hands
reached into the stomach to rip and empty it.
I wanted to loose my gray hair out
upon my shoulders, to feel antlers grow
from bone, letting my own heart be pierced
until the soft pulse shivered in the skin. No.
The dog tore at the deer's throat. And I watched it.
I was the human that could watch it. I was the small,
soul-colored thing that wouldn't change.
The deer trembled and lay still.
It grew slack in the deepening snow.
The road disappeared and the sky turned white.
The snow piled up. It kept on falling.

Yes

It's true: before I left
I used to imagine all kinds of stories
for myself, all kinds of shapes
I could have lived in, the ease of a life
in which perfection is a thoughtless
miracle, or, more simply, the body
of the other man I could imagine
leaving for. One story
in particular returned to me:
seeing my lover at a restaurant with his wife
and two children, watching the way
the wife cuts one child's meat as a waiter
pours water, a group of people laughing
as they stroll past on the walk.
I am not one of those people. I am
somewhere above them, in
and outside this restaurant,
the warm gleam of light that leaps
over glass and spoon, the little candle in its dish
the youngest child reaches for to shake
before he is scolded by my lover
who gets up and walks to the bathroom.
He stands before the sink to wash his hands.
He leans for the soap, the stack of towels,
and I am there suddenly
behind him, no longer light
or witness but a pair of hands
wrapped around his chest,
the hot face pressed into his back.
He turns, without surprise, toward me.
And, yes, everything after.
This is what I dreamed.
And later, punished myself for.
Was there worse that I ignored?
Did I mistake the dream

for excuse to act, was I a liar, heartless,
terrified, was I wrong?
Yes, and yes, and these are the parts of the mind
I do not visit anymore,
certain pleasures and justifications,
the story I might tell myself
about the hero and the conquering
and the journey fulfilled.
My mind has become the lover I do not visit,
knowing the body is not a thought
except it is, knowing that action
is not a thought except it is, the terror
and the joy both generate.
Now, there is only one story.
When the mind asks for it, I tell it, Yes.
I go back to that table and put another face
on the lover, the wife, take out
children and put in statues:
a prince and princess, a rotting apple,
a dragon in its cage. I put myself
at the table. There is the light
on the knife in front of me,
my wife talking absently about herself,
the small disappointments
of being a mother waiting, alone,
for someone else to comfort her.
I am sitting and nodding. I am looking
at my hands that are my lover's:
square and long-fingered and red
at every knuckle. I am eating
with my lover's mouth, I am not listening
with his ears and brain:
I don't know what will happen
when I get up from that table, if I'll find myself
in the bathroom waiting by the tiled wall

with the same sad face each stranger wore
that year, or with a new one, the one
made thin and gray with imagination,
the one of absence and desire.
I turn to the sink and splash water on my face.
I rub my forehead with a towel
as a woman's small hands wrap themselves
around my chest. I feel nothing for them.
I want to be in my own mind now.
I want there to be an end
to dreaming, to this voice that asks
if I want her, if I miss her, am I ready to leave
what's at that table and join a life in which
everything is a reflection of wanting.
Are you ready for the pain? she asks, as if that's
the only thing the mind can ever give us.
Water runs into the lines
of my mouth. It trickles down my chin,
through the beginnings of my beard.
When she digs her nails into my shirt, I don't reply.
I don't ever want to turn and look at her.
I have no idea what I'll find.

Homage for Levis

What angers me now is how
you've become just a story

I struggle to follow, stalking the tracks of birds
in the wind, while the sea and sky

empty around me, their colors showing where everything
must separate and end.

All around is the horizon

and a few branches scattered on the sea
torn apart by churning surf, fragments of earth cast out
like fragments of speech,
a Morse code for a new continent—

Which is a kind of beauty, a kind of starting out.

If you knew me now, you'd see my neighbor
has turned the light on again in his window.
He's always turning on lights, panicking

at curtain and switch, as if waiting for someone

here in your city: where love is harder to achieve
than happiness, it seems. Harder than fame
or a bone breaking. A place

where a man and his wife might drive up to the house
and ask for the hospital a mile away.

Today they had a map, a clean white truck, a bag of food
and flowers. *Please,* the man begged in Spanish.

His map was wrong. And I could see
by the way the woman beside him was twisting and twisting
her shirt ends they'd been driving
a very long while. *Please,*

the man said. How I wish

I had a better story. How I wish
I'd had a translator then, a father like you,
someone pacing all night by the warm light
at his window, so anxious to do right

he would have been, in his own way,
responsible for me.

Tell me what it means to be prepared for someone.

Tell me what it means to look past the poses of envy and fear,
to speak Spanish as if one were fluent,
to look an unknown man in the eye, past his panic
and your own futility, your own incoherent gestures—

In one of your stories, this man and woman would have come
from harvesting fruit down in the valley. Their son
would be the one in the hospital, the one
born here, unlike them, who would be

like you are now, invisible.

The woman, she's maybe ten years younger than her husband.
She looks out the truck window

and I have no idea what she's thinking
as she nods in her rising hopelessness

for her son, who might have been taken
to the emergency room by an aunt or teacher,
who might have as little wrong with him
as an earache that won't quite fade, but this—

simply traveling to him from work—
is enough to show how little she possesses,
the map they've been given—crudely drawn
and all its directions reversed.

Do you know the map you once gave me?

And here I am, still maneuvering by it.

Now I need a destination,
if not an answer. I need a place

in which every kind of story makes sense to me.

The truck stalls in my driveway.
The man and woman listen to my broken Spanish
as a curtain snaps open in my neighbor's window.

For a moment, I can almost imagine this

as a kind of communication,
like the elaborate hand gestures
the first sailors used on their ship,
the boy waving to his boatswain from the crow's nest:

another scrap of sail caught
in the wind, too far past sound, too far past expression and
speech.

He is himself one of the long, dark boats of the West,

waving and waving in
this new haze shape he sees as he strains into the horizon:

one fat branch bobbing in the water, bark curled
and pale flesh peeling. A piece of pine,
a length of seaweed.

First one bird, and then another.

Dragonfly

Not *needle,* but the idea of it. Not *yellow*
but its suggestion
until light penetrates it
or it penetrates the light—

And the one body hooks
into another for awhile,
shivers inside of it over the dead
stem of an iris before rising,

doubled form sheared so suddenly
apart the whole
quivering returns to the individual:
wings almost too thin

to be seen but still
must be believed in,
as the wings of all these others too
must be believed in,

otherwise how would the green
or red or blue body fly,
how hover like the compass point
over the hyssop's

sweet stamens?
How to solidify
this barely imaginable:
to scrape and name and tear

until something inviolable
can be reached,
one point around which
everything else might fix

itself in opposition, calling it *love*
        each time it happens,
pale yellow slivering
        between bay leaves?

Desire is not the essence after all.
        I don't know
what part of me can't be broken,
        what to trust to

when all shapes look the same,
        the rising heat
making each leaf exude the dark
        scent of rot and anise;

what must remain
        when the light shifts
and the yellow disappears, the bright
        fine line dulled back

to invisibility, collapsed
        again into description,
the word "needle," the articulation
        of eyes and wings and legs?

What to believe
        when the creature moves on
and the dimmed petals close,
        the wet dried down to salts

and grit,
        when even the wind
has blown itself away—

Swallow

So ignorant of the world I think it's pleasure first

that makes it dip hallucinatory arcs
across this foggy, close-cropped field
and not the insects wet legs kick up—

Here, and almost here, these

sharp darts that stop me in my tracks: poised, senseless
to its direction
skimming just below, the lingering white

only it sees through and negotiates where I

am less than a stone to it, less than a flea
in the dun belly flashing under the slick blue back—

Wings clip the brief air between us,
scythe the sweet middle of the field where sea mist
seeps its yellow curls, the step ahead and behind me blurred
to the same cold capacities:

somewhere a twist of fence, a scar

of ragged earth a truck tore open
to work itself free.

Dark shank of hair
gleaming in the wet, skin frozen to the bone,

a pair of deer feeding at the wild
last hedge of raspberries.

Closer

The magpie comes and all I can think is
beauty, beauty, though you said
it is a junk bird, though its commonness
makes most ignore it: the blue bands

vibrant against the oil black, the white
chest and belly, the glistening eye
and its feet like rotted arteries branching
off into snow: this is how thin

they are in the world, this is how wretched
and delicate. And the ugly gurgle
at the back of its throat, how it is always
laughing like a broken kettle,

and yet there it is still: *beauty, beauty*
and I am charmed
by what the bird cannot help but do with its long
sweep of tail, its startling accusations

of color: not like the twelve drab quail I've seen
parading the street early evening,
dust-streaked adolescents drunk
from feasting on the neighbor's berries.

They are so fat and stupid these birds,
I cannot love them
for the little comma of feather bobbing
on their heads. I cannot love them

for the way they insist on running
as a means of first escape until,
at last, in one great muffled clap
they rise, and the sound

of their winging is a dull thunder,
        a thousand bed sheets
pulled from the line and shaken together.
        Then I can love them, as I love the garden

with its pockets of stone, forgetting the warning
        others would give of starting
what must be abandoned
        too soon or too late, as we are ourselves

too soon or too late: the problem of beauty
        being how it must be always
distant, observable, taken apart.
        As if preference were all that marked us:

pale ridgelines of grasses darkening out
        into blades of blood—
It would be easier, always, to imagine
        how unlike we are than see

how we have put our own needs in the other's
        mouth. Watch with me. I am the one
who ignores the magpie, garden,
        the commonness of a world that can't

keep its favors secret. I am the one
        abandoning the vision
that preens outside this window, calling itself
        beauty, beauty as if I must name it, as if

I must name you and me
        opposed or part of it:
we are ourselves, always,
        just outside the definition.

If there is a taste,
    a border, a particularity,
then what are we to each other?
    I come closer.

The garden is changing. Fat buds
    spill in the sun, redden greedily at the tips.
Look: another row of poppies opens.
    And in their yellow cups, bees.

ACKNOWLEDGMENTS

Thanks to the following journals, presses, and all the selfless editors who both published the following poems and, on occasion, made them significantly better:

American Poetry Review: "Intimacy"; *Asian American Literary Review:* "Easter in Lisbon"; *Black Warrior Review:* "An Enemy"; *diode:* "The Orchard"; *Ecotone:* "Voyeurs," "Flowers From a New Love after the Divorce"; *Isotope:* "Dragonflies"; *The Journal*: "A Small-Soul-Colored Thing" (published as "Whoso List to Hunt"; reprinted in *Poems of the American West,* 2010); *Kenyon Review:* "Arctic Scale," "Happiness" ("Happiness" reproduced on *Poetry Daily* and *Best New Poems Online*); *Missouri Review:* "Why Some Girls Love Horses," "Yes," "Possibilities in Love," "Closer" ("Why Some Girls Love Horses" reprinted in *Pushcart Prize XXXIV, Best of the Presses,* 2010); *New England Review:* "Feel Like a Little Trepanning Today?," "Tango Lesson"; *Redactions:* "Body of Stuffed Female Fox, Natural History Museum," "Nightingale"; *Utah 'Bite-Sized Poem' videos:* "Swallow"; *Virginia Quarterly Review:* "Ballard Locks"; *Willow Springs*: "Homage for Levis"; *Witness*: "Wax."

Deep gratitude for the art history scholarship of Dr. Lela Graybill, without which "Wax" could not have come to be. "The Orchard" is a response/homage to "Pears" by Robert Hass: thanks to him and his work. Thanks to the keen eyes of Lisa Bickmore, Susan Brown, Andrea Hollander Budy, Kimberly Johnson, Natasha Sajé, and Jennifer Tonge. Thanks to Jeffrey McDaniel. Thanks to grants from the Tanner Humanities Center and the Utah Arts Council. Thanks to the fine folks at Pitt. Thanks to Kundiman and to all my friends and family. Finally, eternal thanks to Sean. I really can't believe you put up with this.